MARK'S MARVELLOUS BOOK

10 9 8 7 6 5 4 3 2 1
copyright © 2015 Alan Mann
ISBN: 978-1-78191-607-0
Published by Christian Focus Publications
Geanies House, Fearn, Tain, Ross-shire
IV20 1TW, Scotland, U.K.
Cover design by Alan Mann and Daniel van Straaten
Illustrations by Alan Mann
Printed in China

MARK'S MARVELLOUS BOOK

Learning about Jesus
through the Gospel

by Alan Mann

MARK'S MARVELLOUS BOOK

Given with love to

....

From

....

For Dad

Contents

Chapter 1:

"pleased"

**with a story from
Mark's Gospel in the Bible,
chapter 1 verses 1 to 11**

Our Dog Dennis

Sometimes our dog Dennis is a good dog.

He gives me a big, happy hello.

He sits when I say "sit!"

Then sometimes he's a bad dog.

He leaves
muddy
foot prints
on the
carpet.

He begs
for chocolate
with big,
sad eyes.

He's a good dog
when he helps paint the fence.

But then he's a bad dog when
he doesn't clean his basket
like he's told to.

And he's very bad when
he drives too fast!

All of us sometimes do good things and sometimes bad things. But there was a man who never did anything wrong.

Many years ago, a man called John spent his time telling people to 'repent', which means to turn away from all the bad things we do and instead turn to God and follow him, because he loves us. John would baptise people who repented. They would be dipped into water as a picture to show that God had washed away the bad things.

One day a man called Jesus came to John to be baptised. John was surprised because he knew Jesus was special and did not need to be baptised. So when John baptised Jesus, something wonderful happened.

God's Spirit appeared in the sky like a dove. God spoke from the sky and said to Jesus, "You are my Son whom I love. I am very pleased with you."

Now, when God says he is very pleased with someone it means a lot! The Bible says that Jesus never did anything wrong, unlike the rest of us. Jesus always did exactly what God wanted.

When Jesus was growing up he did what his Mum and Dad said. He always told the truth. He always cared for other people. He read God's book, the Bible. We cannot be this good, but Jesus was very special because he was God's Son. There was never a single thing about Jesus that was bad. Jesus always pleased God perfectly in every way. So that is why Mark wrote his marvellous book: to tell us about Jesus and how God sent him to put people right, so that one day we can be as good as Jesus and live with God for ever, if we trust him.

Mark called his book a 'gospel' which means 'good news', and that is exactly what it is!

A voice came from heaven, "You are my beloved Son; with you I am well pleased."
Mark chapter 1 verse 11

Chapter 2:

"amazing"

with a story from Mark's Gospel in the Bible, chapter 2 verses 1 to 12

A List of Amazing Things I Have Seen

Thing 1.
A tower of blocks
my baby brother Henry
built last Tuesday.

Thing 2.
A tiny shiny shimmery beetle.

Thing 3.
Animal shapes in the clouds.

Thing 4.
Six snails driving the school bus!

Maybe not... a thing needs to be true
to be properly amazing.

Amazing things make you stop and say, "I have never seen anything like that!" When Jesus came he did really amazing things. So whenever Jesus was around there were lots of other people there too.

One day Jesus was teaching about God. So many people came to hear him that the house was jammed full. Some people outside wanted Jesus to meet their friend who was paralysed, which means he could not move his legs. They knew Jesus could make him better but they could not get through the door because of the crowd. So they made a hole in the roof and lowered their friend in from above!

Jesus was pleased they trusted him and told the paralysed man "Your sins are forgiven". Sins are those things that keep us from God. We sin when we do things God tells us not to do, or when we do not do things he tells us we should do. To be forgiven means God no longer remembers our sins, which means we can be with God. That is the best thing ever!

So forgiving sin was the most AMAZING thing Jesus could have done for the man! Some people there did not think Jesus could do this. They said, "Only God can forgive sins." So to show he really was amazing, Jesus told the paralysed man to stand up and the man stood up! It was a miracle, something that we think is impossible but which God does anyway. The people said, "We never saw anything like this!"

Jesus did really amazing things. He healed people but better still he forgave people their sins, which is something only God can do. It makes you wonder who Jesus is!

They were all amazed and glorified God, saying, "We never saw anything like this!"
Mark chapter 2 verse 12

Chapter 3:

"growing"

with a story from Mark's Gospel in the Bible, chapter 4 verses 1 to 20

The Sower, the Seed and the Soil

When Jesus taught people about God
he would tell stories to help.

One day he told a story about a farmer sowing seeds to grow grain.

The seed fell on different types of soil…

Some seed fell on the path and was eaten by birds.

Some seed fell
on rocky ground
and it grew well
to start with,

but it soon shrivelled up
because there was
not enough soil.

Some seed fell in
the weeds and thorns
and so it died as well.

But then
some seed
fell on
good ground

and
grew strong

and made
lots and lots
of grain
for the farmer!

After Jesus told the story about the sower, the seed and the soil, some of the people who listened to him stayed and asked him what it meant. Jesus explained:

"When God speaks to people it is like a farmer sowing seeds, where the seeds are the words God says.

Some people do not listen to God at all or forget what he says as soon as he says it. That is like the seed that was eaten by birds.

They just say, "NO" to God.

Some people get very excited when they first listen to God, but after a while it gets too hard to do what he says. That is like the seed that did not have enough soil for its roots.

They say, "YES" but only for as long as following God's words is easy.

Some people are too busy with other things to listen to God. That is like the seed that landed in the weeds.

They say, "NOT NOW" to God, "I'M TOO BUSY."

But some people listen to God and believe what he says. That is like the seed which grew strong. They know God better and better day after day, and grow strong just like the grain."

The people who wanted to know God and grow strong kept listening to Jesus and asked him to explain things because they knew he spoke God's words.

We know Jesus is worth listening to. We can still learn about God from Jesus by reading books like Mark's Gospel in the Bible.

"Those that were sown on the good soil
are the ones who hear the word
and accept it and bear fruit,
thirtyfold and sixtyfold and a hundredfold."
Mark chapter 4 verse 20

Chapter 4:

"stormy"

with a story from Mark's Gospel in the Bible, chapter 4 verses 35 to 41

Things that Don't do as they're Told

When I play with my toys
everything happens exactly as I want.

But everywhere else there are
  things that don't do as they're told.

Thing 1.
My baby brother Henry and buttons.

Thing 2.
My flying carpet.

I think it's broken.

Thing 3.
Monsters.

They never wash their hands
before eating.

Thing 4.
The rain!

No matter how hard we try or how big and strong we grow, not many things do just what we tell them to. And it would take a very special person to tell the weather what to do!

This is a good thing. Only God is in charge of everything. Only God is King of everything. That means the sun rises when he says so, trees grow fruit when he says so and even the wind and the seas do what God says.

The Bible says this in lots of places, as well as in a part called the Psalms in chapter 107 verses 23 to 32.

One day Jesus and his friends were in boats on a lake called Galilee. His friends were called disciples.

Then suddenly the wind started to blow and the waves started to grow and a great storm came so that the boats were rolling about and filling with water.

Some of the disciples were fishermen and even they thought they would drown in the waves. They were very scared.

But Jesus stood up on the rolling boat and told the wind and the waves to be quiet and be still. And the wind and the waves actually did what Jesus said! The wind stopped blowing and the lake was calm.

The disciples were absolutely flabbergasted! That means they were so surprised that they did not know what to think.

They asked each other, "Who is he? Even the wind and waves do what they are told when Jesus speaks!"

This was another amazing miracle of Jesus and it makes us all ask "Who is he?"

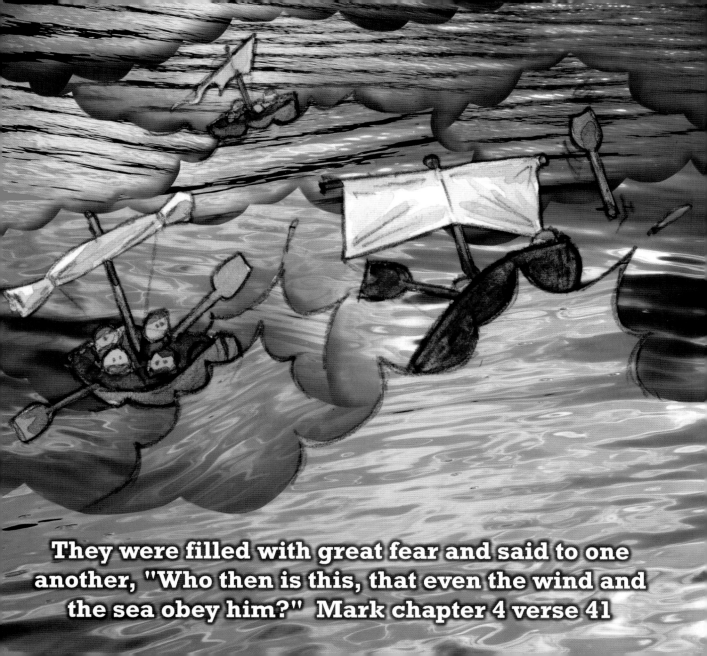

They were filled with great fear and said to one another, "Who then is this, that even the wind and the sea obey him?" Mark chapter 4 verse 41

Chapter 5:

"**hungry**"

**with a story from
Mark's Gospel in the Bible,
chapter 6 verses 30 to 44**

What to Eat on a Picnic

Sally always makes a big pile of
sandwiches for picnics.

We have cheese sandwiches,
and we have ham sandwiches.

Then some sandwiches are
cheese *and* ham,

while some sandwiches are even
ham and cheese.

We have sandwiches with
tuna and mayonnaise,
and sandwiches with
tuna and cucumber,
then sandwiches with
tuna and more tuna.

My sister likes egg and cress
sandwiches,

and I like strawberry jam sandwiches
which need to be left in the sun to get
warm and sticky and lovely.

And then Sally makes one sandwich
with something called
Serrano ham and Manchego cheese and
wild rocket and says, "That one's for me."

But I think I'd like to eat a sandwich
with a wild rocket in it!

Mark tells of a time when Jesus was at a picnic and, as you might guess, it was amazing!

One day Jesus was teaching a big crowd of people, mums and dads, and brothers and sisters. He taught until it was so late that everyone started to get hungry.

Now the people in the crowd had not thought about bringing a picnic. They had just rushed there to hear Jesus. So because Jesus loved them, he told his disciples to get them some food.

The disciples looked at the big crowd and started to count them. There were 1, 2, 3, um, 15, 35, more, 83, 145, phew! 467, 1060, 3192. In the end they decided there must be FIVE THOUSAND! And that was just the men, not counting all the women and children!

The disciples could not begin to guess how they could get enough food for all these people.

There was one young boy who had five small loaves of bread and two small fish but that was all. That is nothing like enough for so many people. So, Jesus did yet another amazing thing.

First he thanked God for the bread and fish and then told the disciples to share the food out to the ginormous crowd. Ginormous means very big.

And as they shared out the food, no one could tell how... but everybody took enough to eat. They were all full up and did not want any more. Not only that, the disciples collected lots of left overs in twelve baskets. Jesus loved and fed all these people, making food for them just like God loves us and makes food for us all the time.

And they all ate and were satisfied.
Mark chapter 6 verse 42

Chapter 6:

"inside"

with a story from Mark's Gospel in the Bible, chapter 7 verses 14 to 23

A List of Disguises I can Imagine

My friend, Geoffrey,
wearing his funny box head.

Polar bears at the zoo,
taking a coffee break.

Our milkman,

who is
really a
space alien
disguised
as a milkman.

Sometimes, when I'm in a park,
I try and decide who might be
secret super heroes.

My apple.

It looked like an apple.

But it was actually
a maggot's house
disguised
as an apple.

It is not always easy to really know what someone is like just by looking at them. We can be different on the inside from what we look on the outside. Some people came to Jesus and said that his friends, the disciples, did not wash enough for God to love them. These people did special washing before they prayed. Praying is speaking to God.

Now washing is a good thing, but Jesus said that God looks at how clean or dirty we are on our insides, in our hearts. That is a lot more important than how dirty we might be on our outsides. That is because what is inside our hearts is who we really are. And Jesus said that from inside our hearts is where all the bad things we do come from. So if clean hands are important, a clean heart is even more important.

He said that we are all dirty in our hearts because of the way we think and the things we want. We need special help to get clean inside, and that is exactly what God wants to do.

Because of all Jesus had done and how he cared for people, we can see that he is clean on the inside. Do you remember how God said he was pleased with Jesus at the start of Mark's Gospel? So it was very sad that others just moaned about how he and his friends washed.

Because Jesus is completely clean inside he can also clean us up, properly clean us up, inside our hearts.

It is God's plan that only Jesus can clean us deep inside our hearts. That is why God sent him, and that is why we need him.

You will see how he does this when you read to the end of Mark's book. If we follow him, he takes all our badness away and gives us all his goodness. It really is good news!

"There is nothing outside a person that by going into him can defile him, but the things that come out of a person are what defile him."
Mark chapter 7 verse 15

Chapter 7:

"lost"

***with a story from
Mark's Gospel in the Bible,
chapter 8 verses 27 to 38***

Things I've Sadly Lost

Unlike my secret packet of crisps…
I know exactly where I keep
my secret packet of crisps.

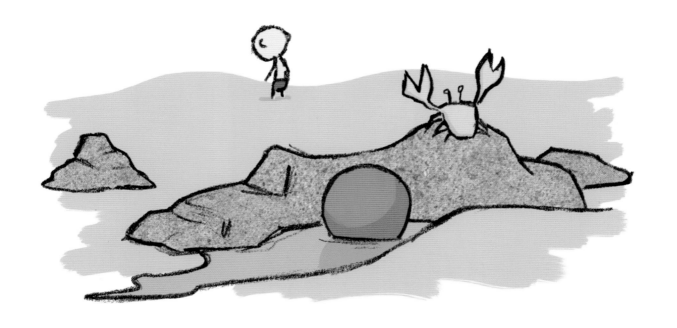

Thing 1.
My most favourite ball.

I lost it on a beach on holiday
and now it's gone forever.

Thing 2.
A pretty flower I found.

I don't know
where it's gone.

I can't see it
anywhere!

Thing 3.

My top secret invisible space ship.

Thing 4. One day we very nearly lost my little brother, Henry, in the supermarket.

That would have been terrible!

Losing things is often sad, but it is very, very sad when we are lost ourselves. After all that Jesus had said and done, one of his friends, Peter, knew how very special he was. Peter said Jesus was the Christ, which means he was the one God had promised to send to save us.

Now that Peter knew who Jesus was, Jesus started to tell his friends what he was going to do.

Jesus said that he was going to die on a cross, which was a terrible thing to happen, but it was God's plan. At that time, a long time ago, soldiers used to put people on a cross to die as a punishment when they broke the law.

Peter did not like to think of Jesus dying on a cross, but Jesus said he had to put God's plan first, and he said that anyone who followed him would have to put God's plan first too.

Then Jesus said something that sounds a little topsy-turvy.

He said that if we put our lives first, in the end we will lose our lives. But if we give our lives away to Jesus and put God first, like Jesus did, our lives will be safe forever.

Our soul is what makes us alive inside. Jesus said it is really important to make sure our soul is safe and not lost. It is more important than anything else we have, any money or things, no matter how much, even if we had the whole world!

Jesus said that after he died on the cross, he would come back to life three days later. What an amazing thing to say! But if you read to the end you will see it is true! And because it is true, we can trust him to look after our souls so that we are not lost.

"For what does it profit a man
to gain the whole world and forfeit his soul?"
Mark chapter 8 verse 36

Chapter 8:

"wait"

with a story from Mark's Gospel in the Bible, chapter 9 verses 1 to 13

Waiting for Sydney to Finish

When Sydney builds something
I try to guess what it is.

"It's a table."

But Sydney just says,
 "I let my work speak for itself."

"Looks like a tower."

"No, it's just not finished yet."

"A man?"
"No."

"A monster?"
"No."

"The Space Alien Kronos,
   Destroyer of Planets?"

"No, I'll do that next."

"It's a crocodile."

"Nearly."

Sometimes we need to wait so that we can understand what is happening. Jesus once told his friends, the disciples, to wait.

A very special thing happened. Jesus and three of his disciples, Peter, James and John, went up a mountain. Jesus prayed to God and then he became bright like the sun. He shone with God's glory. God's glory shows us how wonderful and good God is.

At the same time two men appeared from nowhere. They were called Moses and Elijah. They had lived a long, long time ago and had helped God's people to know God. Jesus talked to them on the mountain about what was going to happen next.

Peter thought that this was great, and he did not want it to stop. So he said they should build tents to sit and talk in. But then God spoke, just like he had when Jesus was baptised at the start. He said, "Listen to my Son." Then Elijah and Moses disappeared and Jesus looked normal again.

So now the disciples knew that Jesus was God's Son, with all of God's power and glory. They could be completely sure, and so we can be sure too.

As they walked down the mountain, Jesus told his disciples not to tell anybody about what had happened until he rose from the dead, but the disciples did not know what Jesus meant.

It was wonderful that God's Son had come, but as wonderful as that was, it was not the whole story. There was something even more wonderful coming that the disciples did not understand yet. That is why Jesus told them to wait. To really know what is happening we have to wait until the end of Mark's Gospel, just like the disciples had to.

And after six days Jesus took with him
Peter and James and John,
and led them up a high mountain by themselves.
And he was transfigured before them.
Mark chapter 9 verse 2

Chapter 9:

"best"

with a story from Mark's Gospel in the Bible, chapter 9 verses 33 to 37

How to be Best in Everything

I must be the prettiest girl ever
when Sally does my hair.

I'm probably
the best ever at football.

Then Sally cleans my boots
so I can play next time.

When I walk Dennis the Dog
I look all grown up.

(Sally taught him to sit when I say "sit!")

So if you want to be the best at something,

we highly recommend Sally.

One day Jesus' friends, his disciples, were talking about which of them was best. This was very sad and rather silly. It was as silly as if Peter said, "I'm tallest," then James said, "I'm best at fishing," and Matthew said, "I can count, best of all," and Bartholomew said, "My beard's definitely the best!"

Remember that Jesus told his disciples not to tell anyone when he shone with God's glory on the mountain? He said that because they still did not understand what he was planning to do, how he was going to save people so they can be with God. If they had understood, they would not have been arguing about who is best.

They should have known better because this happened not long after Jesus told them again that he was going to die on a cross. Jesus had to stop them and put them right.

Jesus said that in his kingdom the most important people are those who spend their time helping others. He called a little child over to them. He said, "It is only people who welcome others like this little child, who really welcome me."

Sometimes we think so much about ourselves that we are not interested in others. We like to think we are too important to care about some people. But Mark's book shows us that Jesus is the most special and important person that ever lived and his whole life was to serve others. Indeed his whole life was to save others!

In God's kingdom, his people think about others before they think about themselves. Just imagine what the world would be like if everybody cared for each other as God wants, and like Jesus did.

And he said to them, "If anyone would be first, he must be last of all and servant of all."
Mark chapter 9 verse 35

Chapter 10:

"impossible"

with a story from Mark's Gospel in the Bible, chapter 10 verses 13 to 31

My Special List of Impossible Things

Thing 1.
Picking up a sleeping cat.

Difficult.

Thing 2.
Balancing
a comfy chair
on the end
of my nose.

Very, very difficult.

Thing 3.

Riding a unicycle on a pelican's beak.

Impossible!

Thing 4.

Walking a tight rope all the way to the moon and back.

One day a man ran up to Jesus to ask him how to get life that never ends in God's kingdom. That would be a great thing to have! Jesus said to him that he had to do all that God had told us to do. The man said he thought he had done all this!

So Jesus said he should give all his stuff away to help the poor and then follow Jesus.

If he did this it would show that he loved God more than anything else and wanted to be with God no matter what. However, the man had lots and lots of stuff and he did not want to give it away.

So the man walked away sad. It was as if he thought his stuff was better than life that never ends!

Do you remember how Jesus taught that everybody has something wrong on the inside, in their hearts? It was in this man as well. He was not as good as he thought he was. That was why he did not want to follow Jesus, but Jesus was exactly the person he needed!

Loving God, as much as Jesus tells us we should, is impossible for us because of what our hearts are like.

Jesus said it is easier to squeeze a camel though a needle's eye than get into God's kingdom! A big hairy camel through a tiny needle's eye!

The disciples were amazed when Jesus said this. Then Jesus said it is impossible for us, but God can do it for us. Nothing is impossible with God.

Jesus came to do the impossible! It is because of him that God can take us into his kingdom.

Mark will show us in his Gospel how Jesus does that.

Jesus said "It is easier for a camel to go through the eye of a needle than for a rich person to enter the kingdom of God." Mark chapter 10 verse 25

Chapter 11:

"promises"

**with a story from
Mark's Gospel in the Bible,
chapter 11 verses 1 to 11**

How to Make a Promise

"Will you look after Bernard
while I'm away?"

"Absolutely, definitely,
without a shadow of a doubt."

"I vow on the life of my plastic shark."

"Cross my heart."

"With a cherry on top."

"Yes or No will do."

"I've forgotten what the question was."

In God's book, the Bible, he tells us that when we promise to do something, we do not have to use special words. Instead, we should just say "yes" or "no" and mean it. (God says that in a letter written by a man called James, chapter 5 verse 12.)

This is exactly what God is like. He always keeps his promises, which means he does what he says he will do.

One day Jesus and his disciples went to a city called Jerusalem for a special holiday. When they got close, Jesus asked them to go and get a donkey so that he could ride into the city on the donkey. When he did this, everybody got very excited and started to wave big leaves in the air and lay their clothes on the ground like a carpet in front of Jesus. They were so happy that they even shouted about it! They shouted, "Hosanna!" which is a way of praising God and means "Save us!"

They did this because they remembered a promise God had made a long time ago when a man, called Zechariah, wrote a book for God. In this book God promised that he would send a king to save his people. And God said this king would ride on a donkey into a city called Jerusalem. (This is in Zechariah's book in the Bible, chapter 9 verse 9.)

So everybody could see that Jesus was the special King sent by God to save us.

God always keeps his promises, and Jesus is the best promise of all. God has promised that if we trust Jesus, he will forgive us our sin and we will live with God forever.

"Hosanna! Blessed is he who comes in the name of the Lord!" Mark chapter 11 verse 9

Chapter 12:

"important"

with a story from Mark's Gospel in the Bible, chapter 12 verses 28 to 34

Important Things I Have to Do

Thing 1.
Feeding Dennis the Dog
is very important,

because he's always
very hungry.

Thing 2.
Brushing my teeth
every night,

because teeth
are most important
for things like
chewing sweets
and
smiling.

Thing 3.

Never

ever

make a dragon angry.

Thing 4.

I definitely mustn't forget Molly's birthday present.

Thing 5.
    And when I go to
        Molly's party
    it is important to wear
        my bicycle helmet.

Thing 6.
    And then Sally
    says I must
        "have fun!"

God has told us what we should do. He tells us in his book, the Bible. (Mark's Gospel is part of God's big book called the Bible.) One day, a scribe, someone who spent lots of time reading the Bible, asked Jesus what was the most important thing God had told us to do.

Jesus said the most important thing God tells us to do is to love him with all we have. God said we should love him with all our heart and all our soul and all our mind and all our strength. Our heart means all we want, our soul means all we are deep inside, our mind means all we think, and our strength means all we can do. That is all we are and have, everything! God says that, in a part of the Bible called Deuteronomy, chapter 6 verse 5.

And Jesus said that the next most important thing God tells us to do is to love others as much as we love ourselves. That means we do not put ourselves first, but care for others as well. God says that in a part of the Bible called Leviticus, chapter 19 verse 18.

Sometimes we can think we are the most important, and that others should always do what we want. But God says that others are just as important as us, and that God himself is the most important of all. He made everything. He is the King of everything and he gives us all the good things we enjoy. So loving God is definitely the right thing to do!

It makes you wonder why our hearts are so bad that we do not listen to him. We really need his help to change us.

"And you shall love the Lord your God
with all your heart and with all your soul
and with all your mind and with all your strength."
Mark chapter 12 verse 30

Chapter 13:

"beautiful"

with a story from Mark's Gospel in the Bible, chapter 14 verses 3 to 9

Another Special List,
this Time of Beautiful Things

Thing 1.

Dennis the dog
is a
very
beautiful
dog.

Even when
he's just been
in the river.

Thing 2.

My personal opinion is that spiders are beautiful.

Thing 3.
Cake in all its various forms
is really, truly beautiful.

Thing 4.

The stars
in the sky
are beautiful
and
the clouds
and
the lightning
as well!

We can have different ideas of what is beautiful and what is not, and sometimes being beautiful means being different. The important thing is to know what God thinks is beautiful.

One day, when Jesus was with friends, a woman came up and poured perfume over him, perfume that cost a lot of money.

Some of the other people there thought that this was just a big waste and moaned about it to themselves, but Jesus said it was a beautiful thing to do.

The woman was really showing how much she loved Jesus while she had the chance, and Jesus knew he would soon die.

Jesus said she did what God wanted, and that whenever people talk about Jesus this story about her would be told as well. (Which is why it is in Mark's book!)

Not everybody loves God and Jesus, but God always notices when people do and he thinks it is a really beautiful thing, no matter what others think.

Jesus said, "Leave her alone. Why do you trouble her? She has done a beautiful thing to me."
Mark chapter 14 verse 6

Chapter 14:

"choices"

**with a story from
Mark's Gospel in the Bible,
chapter 14 verses 32 to 42**

How to Paint a Picture

There are lots and lots of ways
to paint a picture.

You can use paintbrushes,
and put the paint
in all the proper places.

Or you can squirt and splat and splash!

You can paint
a picture
with your
fingers.

Or you can do the full body stamp!

(This is how all the great masters painted.)

There are some things that can be done lots of different ways. But when it comes to putting us right, so that we can be with God, there is only one way. We know this because of a prayer Jesus made.

Prayer is speaking to God. One evening, Jesus went to a garden with his friends, the disciples, to pray.

He was very sad that evening because he knew what was going to happen next. He knew he was going to be arrested, suffer and die. He was going to do this to save us, to get rid of our sin so that we can be with God.

He went further into the garden with three friends called Peter, James and John. He asked them to pray and then went on to pray by himself. He said to God, "Please do not make this happen to me, but not what I choose. Do what you choose."

He was not looking forward to what was going to happen. It was going to be horrible. But God showed him he had to do it to save us.

This is how we know that only Jesus can bring us to God. What happened next was so bad that Jesus would not have done it unless he really needed to. If there was any other way for us to be with God, God would have done that instead. So if God said there is no other way, we should go the one way God has given.

After Jesus prayed, he found his friends sleeping because they were tired. Then some men with swords came to arrest him. They said that he was not doing what God wanted. But we know that he always did what God wanted, even when it was not nice.

And he said, "Abba, Father, all things
are possible for you. Remove this cup from me.
Yet not what I will, but what you will."
Mark chapter 14 verse 36

Chapter 15:

with a story from Mark's Gospel in the Bible, chapter 14 verses 66 to 72

Things that Make Me Sad and Cry

Thing 1.
Standing on snails by accident!

Thing 2.

Getting my
princess dress
all muddy.

Thing 3.

When others laugh at me.

Like when I went
unprepared to
a vegetable
fancy dress
party.

Thing 4.
I cry most when I do something wrong.

When the others were
calling Lucy names… I just smiled.

I like Lucy.

Some people did not like Jesus and what he was teaching, so they tried to stop him. Jesus was put in prison and men asked him lots of questions to try and show he was not doing what God wanted. We, of course, know he was doing just what God wanted.

One of his disciples, called Peter, loved Jesus so much that he followed Jesus to see what was going to happen. As Peter waited a girl asked him if he knew Jesus.

Peter was frightened by what was happening to Jesus so he said he did not know who Jesus was. This happened again and then it happened once more. It happened three times, and each time Peter said, "I do not know him."

Afterwards, Peter felt very sorry for what he had said and began to cry. Jesus had known Peter would say this, even before it happened! But Jesus also knew that deep down, Peter still loved him.

Can you remember what it means to repent? It means to turn away from all the bad things we do and instead turn to God and follow him.

Following God means listening to him and living to please him like Jesus did.

That is just what Peter did. Later, Peter would follow God and not be afraid of men.

None of us have done all that God wants. Do you remember that the most important thing God has told us to do is to love him most of all and love others as much as we love ourselves?

So we all need to repent, say sorry to God and ask God to help us, just like Peter. And God still loves us and will accept us and forgive us because of what Jesus did next.

And immediately the rooster crowed a second time.
And Peter remembered how Jesus had said to him,
"Before the rooster crows twice, you will deny me
three times." And he broke down and wept.
Mark chapter 14 verse 72

Chapter 16:

"cost"

*with a story from
Mark's Gospel in the Bible,
chapter 15 verses 16 to 39*

Things I Can't Afford

Thing 1.
    Sydney's prices when we play shop!

Thing 2.
Big presents!

Thing 3.

My school uniform
that I need for big school.

Thing 4.
A bus ticket to the moon.

Thing 5.   Whoops!

Some things cost a lot more than we can afford to pay, even when we are older and even if we are rich. There are small things we can buy ourselves, and we might be able to save up enough money to buy bigger things. But there are always some things that we can only have if someone gives it to us.

Life with God is like that. God's book, the Bible, says there is a cost to having sin in our hearts. God does not ignore these bad things because he is completely good. God cannot ignore it when bad things happen as if it was not important. The cost of having sin in our hearts is death. However, because God loves us he sent Jesus to save us in a wonderful way.

Remember that some people arrested Jesus. They decided he should die even though he never did anything wrong. When Jesus was around, a long time ago, people called Romans used to kill bad people by hanging them on a cross. It was a very sad and nasty way to die.

This is what happened to Jesus. But when he died on the cross something very strange and important happened. It was the middle of the day with the sun shining, but when Jesus died everything went dark.

It went dark because God was punishing sin in Jesus. That means Jesus was paying the cost of sin. Jesus had no sin in his heart to pay for but he paid for the sin of everyone who follows him.

God is giving us something we cannot afford ourselves. We could never pay enough for the sin in our hearts. However, if we follow Jesus, the cost has already been paid for us by what he did on the cross.

And when the sixth hour had come,
there was darkness over the whole land
until the ninth hour.
Mark chapter 15 verse 33

Chapter 17:

" open "

with a story from
Mark's Gospel in the Bible,
chapter 15 verses 16 to 39

How to Open a Door

When
Sally reads
Mark's Gospel
she closes
her door
so she isn't
interrupted.

We try pushing it open,
but it won't budge.

So we get a pile of books
to reach the handle,

but the door is locked.

Sometimes we shout,
"Ice Cream Van is here!"

But Sally still doesn't come out.

And sometimes we shout,
"Help, Crazy Robot Attack!"

But even then
Sally doesn't come out.

So then
we wait
and wait
and wait
and wait

until
the door
opens
and Sally
comes out
to play!

In the city of Jerusalem, at the time of Jesus, there was a place called the Temple where God said he would meet his people. People would go there on special holidays. But only a few special people called priests were allowed inside the big building of the Temple.

In the Temple there was a very special room, called the 'Most Holy Place', where usually no one was allowed. Only the special High Priest could go in just once each year.

God said that this special room, the 'Most Holy Place', was a picture of him being with his people. However, a big, thick curtain stopped people going in because God is perfectly good. By ourselves we could never be as perfectly good as God is, because of what our hearts are like. So the big, thick curtain showed everyone that there was something stopping them being near to God.

Remember that some people wanted to get rid of Jesus and so killed him by hanging him on a cross, even though he never did anything wrong. This was a terrible way to die, but it was just what Jesus had told his disciples would happen.

A very amazing thing happened when Jesus died on the cross. The big, thick curtain in the Temple was torn in two from top to bottom. God did this to show that anyone can be with him now, because Jesus died to pay the cost of sin.

This is because when Jesus died he took away the sin for everyone who trusts Jesus, so that there is nothing to stop God coming to be with them.

Jesus has opened the door so that we can be with God. This is what makes Mark's book so marvellous!

And Jesus uttered a loud cry and breathed his last.
And the curtain of the temple was torn in two,
from top to bottom. Mark chapter 15 verses 37 to 38

Chapter 18:

" sure "

with a story from Mark's Gospel in the Bible, chapter 16 verses 1 to 8

Things I am Absolutely Definitely Sure of

Cakes are made of magic.

Proof:
Cakes vanish.

Sally's cuddles are safe places.

Proof:
I fall asleep.

Dennis the dog likes to go for a walk.

Proof:

He wags his tail and looks at me
even if I just whisper the word...

It's very windy today.

Proof:
My feet
aren't touching
the ground!

I can write my own name.

Proof: Tabitha

Jesus said he was going to die on a cross so that God could forgive us our sins. Remember that we sin when we do the things God tells us not to do, or when we do not do the things he tells us we should do. Our sin keeps us away from God. But to be forgiven means God no longer remembers our sins. So if we trust Jesus, he will pay the cost of our sin and give us life with God.

But how can we be sure? This is so important and marvellous that we should be very careful to be sure it is true.

Three days after Jesus died on the cross, some of his friends, women who followed him, went to the tomb. The tomb was a cave where his body was put after he died. However, when the women got there they found it open and empty!

The big stone in the door of the tomb had been moved out of the way. There was someone sitting there. He said that Jesus had come back to life. Jesus had risen from the dead just like he said he would! It was an angel, at his tomb, who told his friends he had risen! An angel is a messenger from God. We know this because other people wrote books about Jesus. You can read their books in the Bible too. They were Matthew, Luke and John.

When Jesus rose from the dead, it showed his friends that he really is God's Son and he really did die to save people from their sin. If we trust him, he really will give us eternal life with God. Eternal life is life that never ends and life with God is the best life because God is the best. This is why Mark wrote his book about Jesus, so that we can learn about Jesus and follow him. And this means the story is not finished, but carries on with you if you follow Jesus!

He said to them, "Do not be alarmed.
You seek Jesus of Nazareth, who was crucified.
He has risen; he is not here.
See the place where they laid him.
Mark chapter 16 verse 6

CHRISTIAN FOCUS PUBLICATIONS

Christian Focus | Christian Heritage | CF4K | Mentor

CF4•K
Because you're never too young to know Jesus

Christian Focus Publications

Christian Focus Publications publishes books for adults and children under its four main imprints: Christian Focus, CF4K, Mentor and Christian Heritage. Our books reflect our conviction that God's Word is reliable and Jesus is the way to know him, and live for ever with him.

Our children's publication list includes a Sunday School curriculum that covers pre-school to early teens, and puzzle and activity books. We also publish personal and family devotional titles, biographies and inspirational stories that children will love.

If you are looking for quality Bible teaching for children then we have an excellent range of Bible stories and age-specific theological books.

From pre-school board books to teenage apologetics, we have it covered!